Rosh Hashanah

Festivals Around the World

Words in **bold** can be found in the glossary on page 24.

©2017
Book Life
King's Lynn
Norfolk PE30 4LS

ISBN: 978-1-78637-067-9

Written by:
Charlie Ogden

Edited by:
Grace Jones

Designed by:
Danielle Jones

A catalogue record for this book
is available from the British Library.

Rosh Hashanah

Festivals Around the World

Hello, my name is Jacob.

When you see Jacob, he will tell you how to say a word.

What is a Festival?

A festival takes place when people come together to celebrate a special event or time of the year. Some festivals last for only one day and others go on for many months.

Some people celebrate festivals by having a party with their family and friends. Others celebrate by holding special events, performing dances or playing music.

What is Judaism?

Judaism is a **religion** that began around four thousand years ago in the Middle East. Jewish people believe in one God who they pray to in a **synagogue** or a Jewish place of **worship**.

A synagogue in Hungary.

Rabbi

The word rabbi means 'teacher' in Hebrew.

Jacob says:
SIN-A-GOG (Synagogue)
RAB-EYE (Rabbi)

Jewish people read a holy book called the Torah. The Torah sets out God's laws, which instruct people on how to practise their **faith**. A **rabbi** teaches Jewish people about God's word through the Torah.

What is Rosh Hashanah?

Rosh Hashanah is a Jewish festival that is celebrated for two days in September or October of each year. Rosh Hashanah celebrates the Jewish New Year.

Rosh Hashanah means 'first of the year' in Hebrew.

Rosh Hashanah is celebrated on the first two days of **Yamim Noraim,** which is a ten-day-long festival when Jewish people make up for the bad things that they have done in the last year.

Jacob says:
ROSH HASH-ON-AH (Rosh Hashanah)
YAM-IM NOR-AIM (Yamim Noraim)

Rosh Hashanah is also called the 'Feast of Trumpets'.

The Story of Rosh Hashanah

Rosh Hashanah has been celebrated for thousands of years. Jewish people celebrate the festival every year because it says to do so in the Torah. It is written that on the first day of the seventh month, all Jewish people must have a day of rest.

The Torah says that Rosh Hashanah should fall on the first day of the seventh month. Over time, the seventh month of the Hebrew calendar, called **Tishrei**, became the first month of the Hebrew calendar because it marked the best time of the year to plant seeds.

Rosh Hashanah is also seen as the **anniversary** of the day when God created Adam and Eve. Jewish people believe that Adam and Eve were the first two people created by God.

Because Rosh Hashanah is believed to be the anniversary of the day that God created Adam and Eve, the festival is also seen as a celebration of the relationship between God and people.

Jacob says:
TISH-RAY (Tishrei)

11

Tashlich

For many Jewish people, the most important part of Rosh Hashanah is the **ritual** of Tashlich. This is when Jewish people say prayers near flowing water on the first afternoon of Rosh Hashanah.

Jacob says:
TAR-SH-LICK (Tashlich)

The ritual of Tashlich is supposed to show that Jewish people are washing away their **sins** in the water. This is so that Jewish people can be free of sins in the year to come.

Feast of Trumpets

Rosh Hashanah is also called the 'Feast of Trumpets'. This is because it says in the Torah that trumpets should be blown during the festival.

The main instrument played during the festival is called a **shofar**. The shofar is blown 100 times during Rosh Hashanah.

Shofars

A shofar is a trumpet-like instrument that is made out of ram's horn and it is very important in Judaism. Synagogues often have their own shofars that are only used during special festivals and celebrations.

Shofar

Shofars have a special role in some Jewish festivals. They have to be blown a certain number of times during different prayers and rituals.

Festive Food

Meals during Rosh Hashanah usually include apples dipped in honey. These are supposed to be a **symbol** of the sweet new year to come. A round bread, called a **challah**, is also eaten.

Challahs are a symbol of the cycle of the year.

Gourds

Dates

Jacob says:
HAL-LA (Challah)

Other special foods eaten during Rosh Hashanah include dates and gourds. A gourd is a large fruit with a hard skin.

Prayer and Worship

During Rosh Hashanah, prayer services often take place at synagogues. Religious poems are often spoken aloud during these services. These poems are called **piyyutim**.

Jewish people will often wake up very early on Rosh Hashanah in order to pray at a synagogue. Many people also carry on praying at the synagogue until late at night.

Jacob Says ...

Challah
Jacob says: HAL-LA
A type of bread that is important in Judaism.

Piyyutim
Jacob says: PEE-YUH-TIM
Special religious poems in Judaism.

Rabbi
Jacob says: RAB-EYE
A Jewish teacher or leader.

Rosh Hashanah
Jacob says: ROSH HASH-ON-AH
A Jewish festival that marks the Jewish New Year.

Shofar
Jacob says: SHO-FAR
An instrument that is made from a ram's horn and is used during Jewish festivals.

Synagogue
Jacob says: SIN-A-GOG
A Jewish place of worship.

Tashlich
Jacob says: TAR-SH-LICK
A ritual performed during Rosh Hashanah in order to wash away a person's sins.

Tishrei
Jacob says: TISH-RAY
The first month of the Hebrew calendar.

Yamim Noraim
Jacob says: YAM-IM NOR-AIM
A ten-day-long festival when Jewish people make up for the bad things that they have done.

Glossary

anniversary
a day that is celebrated because an important event happened on that day in another year

faith
belief in a religion and a god or gods

religion
a set of beliefs based around a god or gods

ritual
a set of actions that take place during a religious ceremony

sins
actions that go against God's will

symbol
a thing that represents something else

worship
a religious act where a person shows their love for a god

Index

Credits

Photocredits: Abbreviations: l-left, r-right, b-bottom, t-top, c-centre, m-middle.
Front Cover: bg – Iakov Kalinin; l – natushm m– Four Oaks r – Gregory Gerber. l – bg – Anton_Ivanov; VICTOR TORRES. 2 – Maglara. 4 – Tom Wang, 5 – Noam Armonn. 6 – Ozgur Guvenc. 7 – Anneka. 8 – tomertu, 9– tomertu. 10 – Polyanska Lyubov, 11: main – ArTono; br– BkBook. 12 – Aquarimage. 13 – Dr. Avishai Teicher Pikiwiki Israel [CC BY 2.5 (http://creativecommons.org/licenses/by/2.5)], via Wikimedia Commons. 14 – Tomsickova Tatyana. 15 – david156. 16 – Mordechai Meiri. 17 – Terence Mendoza. 18 – supercat. 19l – Nattika r – Vorobyeva. 20 – Sigapo. 21 – Sean Pavone. Images are courtesy of Shutterstock.com. With thanks to Getty Images, Thinkstock Photo and iStockphoto.